nathan thompson

the
arboretum
towards
the
beginning

nathan
thompson

shearsman books
exeter

Published in the United Kingdom in 2008 by
Shearsman Books Ltd
58 Velwell Road
Exeter EX4 4LD

www.shearsman.com

ISBN 978-1-84861-014-9

Acknowledgements

Grateful acknowledgement is due to the editors of the following journals
and anthologies in which some of these pieces first appeared:

Rupert Loydell at *Stride Magazine*; Ian Seed at *Shadowtrain*; Todd Swift at
nthposition; Tony Frazer at *Shearsman*; Charles Johnson at *Obsessed with Pipework*;
Andy Brown at *The Flying Post*; Peter Philpott at *Great Works*; Dan Waber at
Logolalia; George Ttoouli at *Gists and Piths*; Les Robinson at *Tall Lighthouse*.

Thanks are also due to Luke Kennard for his encouragement, support,
and advice, without which this book would not have got done.

Cover image by David Barker.

CONTENTS

the arboretum towards the beginning

for rain in the arboretum

love song from the arboretum

For Laura

the arboretum towards the beginning

the arboretum towards the beginning

I love that song you always sing in the arboretum

"you chased me down to the apple blossom
where the heart-shaped child offered consolation
in the form of money for cigarettes
but the machine had run out
and the juke-box had no tunes left for me
so I put on my hat and climbed 'a tree (perhaps shrub)'
with a sign on it in a foreign language"

I suppose it was almost entertaining   the sky
warming into evening
like biting an orange on a cold limb

but the child   if I read it right (and who I point out now is not my own)
was getting sad about the arboretum   its lack of leaves in winter

and wanting everything just so   as if his turning into a sleeping lion
while the tree wasn't getting any taller or even looking proved anything
or put distance between
the me in the song and the heart-shape and the potential cola cans
(god I love the potential cola cans   every song should have them)
I have to wonder what it is he wants maybe

          it's not like it's always this way in the park so sorry   sometimes
the tramps sit for hours without anything happening   and I'm
          wondering again
this time about the near miss of the me/tree rhyme in lines 5 and 6
          which is in itself
derivative I think though I can't remember the why and where

in verse two of the song which isn't so memorable
grandma and granddad are turning their face (collective) to the camera
displaying their own not very yellow teeth and saying how things have
    changed
which is what you'd expect   but their mind
will have none of it and looks the other way with an ice-cream   to where
a roundabout is masquerading as a children's plaything and frogs
are not becoming extinct courtesy of a new super-virus
thankfully carried by jukeboxes

                          (the papers say hearts and children
are immune   it's something to do with genetics and the sprawling
connections between disparate things   oh is that child dead?   heart-
attack-shaped and caused by complications to the parentheses

I'll need to try harder on this one   I mean what are the odds
    somebody asked me that this morning   I didn't know quite
what to say   which seemed to be the right answer
      but left me defenceless in this arboretum
where it's widely believed a child's death is unavoidable

a pile of apples slumps from a market trestle

the air today is so malleable

an amanuensis for water

you could almost write Keats on it with your finger

a walk with the narrator

he said the roses wouldn't come out
in the city this year   there's too much
already to be done   pull up a chair
we'll talk about it

you are home and the grass is growing
between the tulips   and at least
this isn't a place god comes to be bothered
except on Sundays

                    even the cathedral windows
have been blown out and it is filthy with light
the fighting tarnished gargoyles are losing their teeth
and I feel like a child being told everything about love
the strange shared frankness disgust wonder
but lacking narrative until narrative is imposed

over there a girl is saying thank you to a daisy
for its simple effort not realising
its sovereign guilty secrets   e.g. its flower
is a busking hat for bees and if her mother knew
she wouldn't let her talk to it

the sky is taking on a Gregorian aspect
of shared experience
                    while the last crows gather their stuff

the air is cooling as they've demanded all day

solstice

collateral   processed

       it is a line drawing

corona surrounding a candle

witch this   stick hazel

       stunted forest echoes

fingers broken   lichen covers the boulders

what's to check   swallows

       waiting granite seams

hair left behind   whose footsteps

Pentecost

her loom the belittlement of silver

the old tin cans buffering communication

across a tennis court

wintering without nets   coal is hibernating

like a jewelled toad
                    ornate as the janitor
of our lady

a grounds-man measures trees by their weddings
                                        it seems none
have sprouted a crucifixion or were rolled by picts

some however caught in a garter   and spick and span

themselves over skylines

maybe Friday or Saturday

who shining summer

owed more on the river

                 a child would be

catches tiny fish

    benefitting from the sun

a camouflage   this is all the distance

something is missing from   a magician
has left his wand behind   there'll be no doves

I am dipping my toe in the water
it is cool and sickly

            this is not encouraging

the banks rubbed clean and grassy
      somebody should be on them
openly flaunting

purloining a fritillary

squeezed from a tube commercially skipping hair and legs to a
                                                    fairytale ending

each wing-beat is an anticipation of a last step back in advertising

she is as elusive as tinnitus

drift

it's half past ten new summer time
not the conventional midnight ceremonial
and many of the things I think are true are in fact not
for instance

       'fall'

is the English word for autumn as developed
in the 16th century   autumn only reverted
in 1800 but that's not it   it's unseasonal

               your love
she is extraordinary like a stalactite pointing
the wrong way but still labelled 'a stalactite'
for some scientific reason you don't understand
and she is sitting right here in all this weirdness   whose
metaphor is   'it's none of your business'
I'm not claiming waves for the wheat-fields here

             it's just   you say
I've taken a walk to the wheat-fields
and with your love have founded a whole new aquatic ecosystem

you're damn right it's marvellous
considering the earlier cavernous darkness
filled with unpigmented life-forms
that have white feathers instead of limbs

there's nothing
artless about these spring colours masquerading as sentences
they're here   look   the quaint lilac sea-horses
chewing around larks' nests
for the secret to melody

so they're not asking much
after all this will be a love song if they find their secret   maybe you'll
accept it

colluding in wine

splayed between
                pushed out like butter
spread in a garden flecked over the grass
                             there is no story to speak of

biodynamically the time is right and nothing much unusual under the
                               moon
the men treading huddling in sunglasses after the event   refusing a
                                         cigarette

a few questions from the city

out of things I don't understand one
is belligerent waves of casuarinas
unseasonal and invisible
engaging with or against a taut theory

where is the spyware I bought from that internet site dignified
by a 'why bother' recommendation in a national paper

it was articulated in the back pages just the same
an advert in blackly visible ink large print

that was weeks ago now   it implies 'water
is the casual theme today' and catching it
during a children's programme   the screen welling up
like an eye too busy to bother

                    (and these moths
round a candle in the rain threatening
to extinguish it   can they even fly in this weather
and why hasn't the wind . . .)

                         I know   I know
but germination happens just the same and frowns a little
with concentration as the shoot breaks through
like a fascist idea with so many ideas around it

what will follow   music perhaps and a choice of narratee
     a museum at night where nothing comes to life and yet
nobody feels secure

                    maybe I should leave
something outside it for you   buried treasure
to turn your head when you pass the spot and
nobody will know what you're looking at

but you'll think of me until you forget to
and I forget too   I wish I could remember that was you
was it that you

instead I am fishing for data
at the advertising agency where I found
something once

        such as waiting for the rain to stop so that paddling
will become universally approved of again

        and I can fly a kite in the arboretum
without being laughed at   when birds come out
like glorious transvestites in a club called *Minkies* and call you honey and
you like it   thinking of that saying   'wearing your cuff on your sleeve
   is a sign of hope'

casting calls are almost complete

the black cat in the arboretum is to be played by a black cat

because out of all the applicants she was by far the most beautiful

variations

if the sky is almost blue because it is raining
does the art of difficulty continue to clarify
you are sailing across it
     'who are taller
than asking questions' but stoop grammatically
which is metaphorical since in the world
your height could not be described as dramatic
but there are echoes
    in the sweet shell
that prints a kiss
on the envelope
of a letter you will write
tomorrow unaware of the contents until you open it

★ ★ ★

the black cat said as she smelled the air
how should she place the button on the table
in character next to
  caught like this response to solitude as
'something in the teeth'
     a gas fire
heavy and nervously serious who is picking up this look
to read
    I will avoid
the humorous endorsement it is not my eye

if she were to play with all the other things on the table
what would it make more than
'ingots are best wrapped in paper' safe
from prying psychics am I to be a ghost
or has she not seen me yet

★ ★ ★

who opens the piano seat
and the walls of Jericho tumble

to my ears it was always wolves
I will try not to bore further but I liked the effect
of the right pedal more than the left
is this relevant

* * *

I am   now   your hands are   too far
for agreement   if this were autobiography
it would be shy people talking over one another
what should you

'this is the wrong way to say anything'
anyone still listening   the wind in the trees

service

mellifluous rituals in the dark

a violin spurting a bunch of hoe-downs   happy as a full vase

and winter steaming off the corrugated roof singing and rattling   a
    kettle on a ringed hob

projection digressions

I'm riding the slow service
and we're going to pass
the 8 wonders of the developed world
                                    look
an egret   they're new here aren't they
and neat except for that back-quiff

mist off the river anchors us
and grapples with movement   (what
do you think of that train-spotters
it must be a relief not to need to be so precise)   but this is the
        free jazz train
and this is a technicality

                        say for example there's a clue
in the crossword you'd get but I won't
involving the indefinite article
and a psychological equation for poetry   where are you then

the mist is clearing allowing for some hills
to recede from me

                        remember the way you loved me backwards to this
        point   it was prosaic

here's your anagram   leporet   clue   snow hares
would be clearly visible even though it's winter   dunces
taking the world on solo and so fast   but who am I to judge I'm no critic

listen   the conductor has a purple rose in his lapel
as this is a special occasion
                            and he smiles as he checks my ticket
without grudge   he must be missing somebody terribly
to be so polite

                    I'm still moving away
from those hills like an irreversible chemical reaction
(now is that copper sulphite poisonous sir   it smells
of mango chutney (the trumpeter's little (musical) joke   it doesn't))
        can you
tell the coda's swinging

                        it'll all be over by the time
we reach the tunnel   I'm looking forward to that
as anyway I've forgotten my glasses
and I'm missing all the wonders for you   thanks god
for making that egret so big and so close
it was almost an atmospheric change
or I'd never have detected it

                        the saxophone
varies where we're going and lots of passengers
have got frightened and got off at the last stop
                                        but I like you
and I'm weary of destinations and increasingly wary

snow parks simply

like birdsong lounging   drawn out and pricked and white   as if
you could hold it cupped in a glass and wait for the glass to break
in your hand

the crystals are like shadows   and vary their form starkly   part full
to part empty as if a matter of choice with the light

their little business of melting throws sponges sifting heavily from the
trees like the feeling of overstuffing your mouth with marshmallows

for a spoon propelling sugar people often forget that many others die
in the snow

this one was always in the balance

for rain in the arboretum

for rain in the arboretum

sunlight over the arboretum
has the same   as rain

                not cold
cleansing   but greenhouse weather
and the aviary is alive with skits of water-song

has somebody made a mistake today
          it must be a comedy Englishman
for it to be about the weather
                              but first thoughts are not always . . .

ghosts of children flitting between branches
on the wings of birds   so tired and crazy
for a night in   heaven seems to be
getting narrower   what with half-kisses
missed and guilty   feather litter   which isn't an insult
      perhaps you'd like to say something now
this is your place to say it . . .

Aquarium

The arsonist has been terrorizing our village for a year and three days.

So I have challenged the arsonist (the villagers do not know if it is a he or a she) to a competition. One of the few buildings left standing is the aquarium, internally hooded in water.

If I can burn it down before him he will cease his campaign. This is kept secret from the other villagers. Silence is the arsonist's price.

There are certain inhabitants of the aquarium, such as mussels and lobsters, who seem predisposed to nervousness. It is as if they have seen it all before in genetic visions stretched across the inside of their putative foreheads, flickering weeds conjuring silt from the mouths of rivers in a storm.

My oil slicks their water calmly as a disaster, and though it is late there is no sign of the arsonist. Maybe I have jumped him and our village will be saved (except for its tourist economy).

For everything but me and perhaps the arsonist it is dark under the oil in the aquarium when I light a match. It goes out. But the second one doesn't, and I am surrounded by ghostly silhouettes of exoskeletons and slabs of expectant eyes. I am hopeful.

If this doesn't work, and it didn't last time or any of the times before that, tomorrow it will be the font museum.

Lucy's Aural History

I

The class of '97 avers my fate is in their hands. I point out there is something wrong with that sentence but they continue to prosper. "Boy, do you suffer," says the pigtail kid, who now only has the ghosts of pig-tails denting her aura, "I ought to get my father on you."

Her dog is setting under the table because it is that kind of dog: it likes the glint of sunlight on silverware. We are approaching the right time and a little bell rings, the sound ogling kitschly in the nearby twilight.

"Here, let me help you," I say.

II

For our task of reintegration we are to bond while undressing a mannequin, trying not to appear disappointed. The pigtail kid insists that her bicycle is helpful and good for morale. "It will pass the time more quickly," she says. I start on the 39 buttons and am struck by the thought of a carnation, 'how green; how edible,' but I do not share it.

"Your glasses are steaming up," says the pigtail kid, whose name I now remember is Lucy, "and you're not even wearing glasses." It is possible she is sweet on me, but I don't know if I could ever love her. "Anyway, you're married," I say.

Lucy ignores me: "Can you keep the noise down please, I'm trying to concentrate." Her bicycle hums figures of eight, increasingly leanly. You couldn't put a hair between Lucy and the mannequin.

III

We eat the reunion dinner under the table. "It works better that way," Lucy explains, "you don't get so sad when the moon comes up and the day is over."

I drop a green olive and it rolls to Lucy's feet. It looks like a tiny mournful moon. "You ruin everything," she says.

IV

Returning from the reunion on a stolen bicycle I wonder what happened to my life. Whether I should have dotted more Ts or shaken my head more often.

Something like a large larynx wells in my throat. It is an orange Lucy painted her face on for me and told me to swallow whole, saying "Now you will always be happy."

Mary-Jane

Punch-line

Mary-Jane abdicates to find the purely empty space she is currently filling. In the strictest terms she is an imaginary event hollowed to a silhouette correlating surrounding junk. I am concerned about the effect this will have when Mary-Jane tries to hug me or stoops to pick up a mouse; the mouse I have loved since he occurred to me beside a black container that cannot be contained. The mouse is, in this respect, the exact conceptual opposite of a Russian doll. I take Mary-Jane's spirit-level but now I find only Mary-Jane in the bubble, which she measures with what used to be her sides like the insults of dead people. Mary-Jane admires herself as a picture-frame you can walk through spelling 'goalposts,' 'now,' and 'soft-focus'.

Missing Mary-Jane

Mary-Jane would be obsessed with the corners of my eyes. "Where did you get them, the corners of your eyes?" she'd say if she could.

"You know, Mary-Jane," I splutter one day, as young men do, "I wish you'd stop staring at me like that with the whites around your irises. It makes me feel all godless and nondenominational."

She would stroke my bald patch. The underside of a breeze sucks up its moisture.

"Your problem is you try to combine a capitalist progression with communist values. The resulting discord, should you ever sound it, would undo 4'33". You are a vandal, but you do not practise enough for it to ever happen." That's the sort of thing Mary-Jane would say.

Maybe Mary-Jane used to be good at diagnosing spiritual crises. There is such elegance under her thoughts, like a diving bell.

Adoptions

My finch has a pink ring attached to one leg. She is dead and gone as the spots of a ladybird in winter.

Blood at her bill has drained the rare masculine colour from her plumage as if the weather never mattered.

Our empty conservatory is, surprisingly, flecked with rain. Lines drop like the remnants of a picture.

"God holds children and loud noises very lightly though a chalice may quiver at the lips," I explain.

I have never wanted there to be angels more.

The letter licks the table. It is like sticky hair and I must look to it again, though its style bothers me.

All is forgiven

Mary-Jane does not want a glass of water so I drink it for her.

"I came close to being mortally injured by water," she tells me, "in a past life." Should I encourage this return to form?

"What's it like, having a past life, reincarnation, that side of things?" I wonder aloud, but Mary-Jane is not listening. She dislikes the present tense.

"One thing I should tell you," says Mary-Jane "is that reincarnation means being unfurled petal by petal. From a lily it becomes more purely someone ignoring a stained-glass window. When you are reincarnated you let in light and feed strange pigments to the birds, who claim immunity.

This is because birds are full of understanding. Otherwise they would fly through windows by themselves and skew dartboards long before they were even looking for them. You make me quite queasy talking this way. I am so jealous of birds and lilies."

Mary-Jane is empty of tears, and I would comfort her.

Isabel: A Novel

i.

My love Isabel has invented a new primary colour. It will be added to the spectrum in a ceremony on Sunday at which a rainbow will be cut and the colours tied by a vasectomist.

The vasectomist is very proud of Isabel and stands in awe of her creativity. "Were it not for your height," confides Isabel bashfully, "I should never have foreseen this colour."

Experiments are being conducted to discover the weight of Isabel's new colour, but Isabel will have nothing to do with them. Isabel sees herself as an artist.

ii.

Tomorrow is Saturday so, as usual, I am taking Isabel to the pictures. Recently Isabel has found the experience less stimulating than she used. This is why she has asked if she can bring the vasectomist.

I am against it as last time he sat between us and prevented us seeing one another because he is so tall, but Isabel insists and it is her treat. As she says, it's not every day you discover a new primary colour.

By way of a concession Isabel has agreed we will see a black and white film; I always find them less demanding.

iii.

The vasectomist arrives first, wearing a novelty hat that looks as though he picked it up in a bar. I get the impression he is trying to impress Isabel, who lives for new things. He claims it is just his hair, which seems unlikely.

When Isabel turns up late she is glowing in a dress made entirely of her new colour and gleaming like an animal from the Song of Songs. I am concerned that she will reflect onto the screen and spoil the film, but do not say anything.

"I like what you've done with your hair," she says to the vasectomist, beaming. "It looks almost as if you're wearing a hat. It would be an easy mistake for an unimaginative person."

I think I detect pity in the vasectomist's eyes but it could be lust. It is hard to tell from this distance and I admit I can't understand his eyes. But Isabel is a preview, and he is not the only one staring.

Next time, I decide, I will arrive last.

iv.

It turns out that tonight's screening has been cancelled owing to lack of interest and that instead Isabel is to give a paper on the theology of beer. I did not know that Isabel had ever thought about the theology of beer but she is very versatile and we applaud her, both of us, in a moment of manly comradery for the cameras.

The lights dim and you can no longer see Isabel's colour.

"Beer," she begins, "is a green ashtray representing a hint of lime. We can trace this zest to monastic breweries and monks who catapulted beer to fame at combustible strengths, converting many."

Someone coughs. Isabel is an odd choice to replace *10 Megaton Charlie* but that's the nature of celebrity.

"Likewise," Isabel continues, "beer often involves animals, including bishops, and thrives on their eccentricity, teeming with interest like medieval spit to modern science. This makes beer preferable to water, which is all but silent. And explains why Marxists value water over bishops."

Isabel pauses and the vasectomist and I agree that she is very clever, though prone to be obtuse. But the crowd is restless and I am beginning to worry about Isabel, who tries a change of tack.

"The beer mat developed alongside the cat show. Engineered to be still, the English breeds would lie on their backs in pubs and clasp pints in their paws to prevent spillage. Cats have seen humans in their cups and behave accordingly."

There is no applause.

v.

I am the last person in the cinema. The audience is not impressed by Isabel's talk and leaves doubting her ability to create a new primary colour even though she is wearing one. It is still dark in the cinema when the vasectomist too leaves in disgust.

This is sad as Isabel and I weren't going to have a baby. It was the only idea of mine she ever liked.

And now that he's gone I rather miss the vasectomist. I don't expect we will see him again.

When we get home, Isabel takes off her new colour and hangs it in the wardrobe to be forgotten by our grandchildren. I am being honest when I tell her I have always thought she was more beautiful naked.

The Arsonist's Holiday

You passed me on the road out of Mandalay. There had been some kind of mix-up with the traffic lights, as if they were fires in entirely the wrong place burning the scalps off tourists dealing through reputable agencies.

I was ready for disappointment and you were obliging, refusing even to play with the flying fish who were so eager and so sad. I can only put it down to chance, this failure to see the elemental side to their predicament.

And that's why your ring is not on my finger—though like all mermaids you were beautiful. The Xeroxed ice-bergs plaguing your childhood melted at my fingertips like the foppish blithering of the night sky which, I suppose, still pocks at your ceiling nonchalant as sea-birds.

I slipped out of the water before dawn, loveless and surprisingly far from land, clutching a laminated brochure.

. . . I see you've wasted it   all a matter of timing
like managing to become and be a butterfly   how did you
train your eyelids to do that
                              breaking butterflies

but of course you can't hear me over the sun
(and the church is abolishing limbo
                              which seems arbitrary)

all the same there is a fountain here
where water goes to die   the drops
are tiny indulgent elephants
                              spinning and making 'whoopee'
faces as they tumble

                  this is as close as we get today
and too artful and not animal enough
                        its embarrassed cough is rather masculine
which isn't at all what I asked for

love song from the arboretum

laws of attraction

the day you stole that harmonica
was the first day of the rest of my life

                                                   I wish
I could understand the colours you blow
that wave on the frequency of night-lilies
collating what they dredge

                                   sweetening the philistine edges
of your dimly lit ornamental music

I expect the frogs will be at it for some time
winking like ellipses in brilliant prose

arguing an eloquent case
                                for misplacing adjectives knowingly
sequentially

smudging the corners of our real riverside sheets

answers on a post-card please

the cathedral bell left like a cat yawning
     a sunken city   the walls are moon-wash
       I believe you there has been no rain today
though May is the month for rain not April
the songs are wrong and is that comforting

if you take this and divide it appropriately
you are left with   I am glad that the weather
is unseasonal   it's majestic and lots of other
unreasonable words   meaning   sleep is disturbed
and yet
       if I'm honest it's somewhere in-between
this and the dream I had   I had to rescue you
from a hospital because there was an insomnia epidemic
at the prison   the only way to reach you was through the cafe
but 'they' were reluctant   I suppose it could become less possible
considering   what I want now is to be able
to say I love you and not be laughed out of form
for writing a sonnet   could things get more referential

let's take the ego out of it   and yet
knowing   this   is the way   forward   if you're listening
guess the quote marks   there is a great calm
fins pop out of
       "I'm taking away the compliments now
don't bother me"   why do you always hate them
what else am I supposed to do   how to appear green
and be really innocent which this is I'm not joking

     I've followed this and I'm in pain   "have a drink"
"no thank you"   "no"   I think I need
to understand   you'll move some of your anatomy
maybe all of it   which at least is beyond

the bells have a colour all of their own   copper
left out in deep snow   more brittle than green
and they're trying to juxtapose something without committing robbery
          it makes them weep   which is private when no one is about
who is certain   (it's about time I remembered
not to tell you I care   you don't like it)

above your room the fallacy of the cat let upstairs
is tinkering with her canaries   she is in
a position of power   we lack the glossy element of primary colour

"the bells"

or   are we shooting today   if so   it makes
no difference   I'm off duty and forgive me   do you
understand   do I   do   perhaps I shouldn't take this
much further   I must be trying your indulgence
with my patience   the moon is simply aching
and something upstairs has been hit by somebody advancing

but because your grateful palace is so tender
there are no tramps holy in the street tonight
which is naive   possibly offensive
you sleep so quietly you are almost a picture
and still time passes   there is no now to this
without a concerted effort to be learning

my faith in such quietness may be dismissed as ignorance
as a shell is still and empty   sounding in this tidal river   is it too late now
to take back the consequences or a drink   and is that
not humble   it's pompous to talk this way
when the stars are making their enquiries round the streetlamps
     a little matter of moth-man-ship that can seem terribly important
through the window   rolling and knocking like bone dice
on a solid table   curtain-blind and not at all opaque

perhaps you can't answer why it is you're so quiet
and so not absent   yet present is not right
in this distant shadow of the cathedral   maybe
you could believe that love   and so   but yet
          a charcoal parcelled drawing of the night too

I don't need the answer but want is a different word
in the Profound Dictionary of Happiness   and enough
is   complete   and   satisfied   which is really not ironic
     'I want' and yet 'I am complete' in the smallness of your breath
I will make sure nothing can harm your happiness
with its whispered wing-beats
                                        because I can really say
I am happy   or   my heart skips   and there's not anything
silly about it or broken   the lucky footsteps in the street
follow mine about on the pavement   maybe the 2nd wise man's shadow

but it is no threat as the light enters and several hours
of missed bells with the substitute dawn chorus of canaries
     (it seems we shall have to get a new cat   a better one)

there are secrets to tell and your eyes not even open yet
to know   why is there still an ache   do I have
a condition   it is enough and all I want is
that you are happy   no questions   nothing gilded except mischief
          but not like wars or terrorists or even nuisancists
stealing the bangs out of Christmas crackers   there's no need
for any of that   just our sonnet-like flexibility
and protracted/unprotracted unity under your unfeasibly late mistletoe
          all we need and
                              all we want is . . .

but maybe I am thinking for you   turning us into a tourist trap
and this is not a brochure   which is kind of problematic

I think it's time now   but pigeons are always welcome
I like their morning messages   they sound of you

first morning
                last morning   it's really good that you're here
    the waters are simply amazing this spring   so opulently wine-like
        here   you too   take some   hold our hands   please   be
our guest

Remembering Lee Harwood's 'Love in the Organ Loft'
Exeter, May 2007.

come to the arboretum with me

likening to
                             strophic nights
from blame under the grey felt roofs
inhabiting all those taxis

                       to your later arch with a realist's touch
not to one   though there's an irony in this
convoluting my sentences

I am beginning to believe you
now you say you lack structure

which is why the clowns are so sad
spinning plates of substandard grievances
on sticks of rock from somewhere they never wanted to go

that's just below your lower lashes
where a grey-blue emphasis could flick a fall
into the ideology of 'will-power'

in answer to your earlier question I feel that the trees are growing wetly
outside the window   which isn't very profound
but is comforting
                  more so even than watching you
and more hearing you   sleep snore flirt with speech

and yes   I'm wrong   this is profound   bringing with it
a desire for windmills and bright paintings of drab things
to try and make up for all the world's past topiary

and since you asked once

         I'd say that should you wake up soon
I'll tell you   if we went to the zoo instead tomorrow
and saved you up like a gag in front of the pandas' cages
it's possible we might all just stand a chance

enjoy

someone came home the other day
    I forget   a discursive bowl of flowers
        petals floating under   I wake up

to swallows   'me too'   there has been
    much discussion about this
        in the shelter of rooftops

stolen presents plural of now
    explain to journeys how to proceed
        turn about the cathedral widdershins

who is shrinking out of favour
    if you are lonely
        wrap up warm or something   the petals

creep around the bowl pretending to be art
    so distant   including how to make
        a perfect cup of coffee implode   'the tip of your tongue'

in another
    a small bird flies in one window
        out the next   does it mean more

a big one does the same
    should it be   a butterfly
        casual with so much fragility

the table remaining frozen
    ill chosen   on a startled carpet
        'anachronism'   question: to join the mistletoe

Pilate never finished his question

      the possibility in our window
a final act of music infusing
the arboretum's sappy jugular

something moves in the green fading
we'll never know

             condition of evening approaching
narrative   who's that smiling   your clothes
feel so good against you   they must

and 'far away' a clock is baking to chime

a glance wouldn't hurt   so
burgeons   in a window box
stashed with kudos and orchids

perhaps this will spiral in a minute into long sentences

in the meantime I am content to wait
imagining myself ashtray debris sorry
between your wing-beats   "silence

is so companionable"   you had to say this
to overflow more convincingly

tracker action

I think there's a migration here
the magnets are going a bit haywire
a vandal reversed the poles and the ley-lines are fucked

do you think you could find it in your anatomy
to forgive this caprice

                    it's 3 in the morning
and I'm tired   which may seem prosaic
but because I mean 'I love you'

                  I thought I just heard
someone shouting help outside the window
but I was mistaken   they seem ok
I'm just nervous with the drum's vibration

perhaps it's possible you're thinking similar
this town's been caught in lesser geography
and pawed its way out   I'm mincing my words
and I don't think you approve of this partial bravery

after all it was you took my hand
and took me looking for geese
chasing the garden path wildly   take the countryside

does anyone really love it bar the addicts
whooping show-tunes to cliff-sides facing
interrogation as to their intentions

                    the stars are bursting
like a joke out of a can without a deadline
and you seem to be using my name for something

should I sue you all the way down the street

because   through the base of a horizon
I'm not sure you'll make much sense of it
having somehow lost your way   (in a book about rabbits

there wasn't a single rabbit   just a photocopied memo
saying 'no rabbits' and 'keep off the grass'
with something of 'if you know what's good for you' about it)

    there's a big moon thankfully
we're going to need it   remember I said 'I love you'
it's like a sail and maybe not quite enough

for a pale thank you   dream this telegram made it to the arboretum
and there's a real it matters about the situation

moon song

trying to fly a-physically like that kite
your father nearly bought you and lost the string

you're still towing it now   it clinks
over the cattle-grids   god knows what it's made of

speaking in a foreign accent you open your chocolates
because it makes you feel more surprised that way

too much movement can be dangerous
depending on context   'I pledge to you

the poorly remains of my honour'
says the man

'I can't help feeling this stolen harmonica
is a pilgrim naked in the headlights'

notes   very particular

because   the sunflower in the picture
is   only a sunflower   not even
    sun not flower not perhaps
very good picture I don't know

its leaves   the only thing
    away to the sea-side
this   heat
take your hair in my hand and whisper

"oh, we could have known"   a pen
        comfort touch   written on
white on blue   white horses
otherwise   calm

                I am sorry
you haven't   today
or rather   touch   the archangels
    put down their harps   their wings

    which one
is most   few clouds
        all that blue

what a day out

'what else' is there not to say
I haven't broadened the vocabulary of your eyelashes
and the plant pot maybe still smells heavenly of roses
          (this is a memory of a purple one
I bought you at the arboretum for your favourite colour   opaque
and delicious)

I can't remember what leaves tomorrow or why
and I don't know where it's going or who'll be on it
except that contractually it's bound to involve the moon
and a cold-sounding rhyme
          in the meantime can I have the line of your hips back please
and the smooth of your hand   thank you
                                        will you keep them safe for me
not that I'm   even your lips

'in the meantime' is the setting for this day out
shall we borrow a small house and talk in country dialects
or should it be more simply urban
with window baskets and canapés of salmon sunsets
probably farmed ones   then again maybe somewhere fabulous
like the arboretum

not today   a theme park   I'll keep to the point
we're on all the rides (well one over and over)
and we're dizzy eating happy junk with added serotonins
                                        screw up your eyes
that cola bottle could be a max-speed avocado we're so high

see those plastic lions risking down a one way Jurassic street
this could be our favourite
though it seems we've missed a turning somewhere

for any of this to happen realistically   let's say
                         'it was a good day out' all the same

whenever you are tomorrow it doesn't feel back where I started

channelling the spirit of pirate Paul Evans

you know it's been good   when
'all night' is closed

and to those trees next to each other
    can they be so different   by moonlight
insomniac catatonic and still in agreement
leaving your house
               the child
who asked for a green pen as it was
a treasure-hunt on pirate day
made us king and queen of the pirates
not a romantic swiz in range
     the supernatural seems a bit poorly
if you follow

        it's up to your ears
waking to compensate for an eye-patch
any formal agreement nomenclature for the moment
    this is yours for stillness   breathing life
into the dummy waiting at the end of a ruined pier
naked save for his own voice

in another version   I met you
plying the one-armed bandit with holy signs
in a second-hand shop   where you'd dropped your beads
I helped you pick them up   like rewinding
film footage of rain moulded in ice-cream scoops
or somewhere in between   who'd not have lightened
around this just shy of mythology   falling between
the wood-knots emulating letters pressed
skull and crossbones in the table

it wasn't really a second-hand shop   it was
a pub you go to just to meet someone called

to bring shame on Petrarch   so kind of literary
    easy to tell because the clientele wore hats
to smudge their relationship with posterity
which thinks the chairs are nice
when the world is empty and grateful

I don't think we thought
between the trees' fey arm-wrestling
    these times are when you need help in the crows' nest
to set aside mind-space for grandma and granddad

but no-one will die if you don't finish
knitting this song   nor if you do   it's more like a flag
perhaps the way it might make us a little

sonnet for a book about stained glass

how to understand the concluding   god
the immaculate puller of heart-strings
      but yes I'm with you   as with the longed
out of bed breaking bread in the morning
            did you read in the newspaper   last night
ten men at least dreamed in this town   alone
among them   I found you   (not obstinate
as such)   I guess   just lucky   nine heteronyms
also found you   making up the number
performing its shape greenly   among the hills
surfed by motes under astonished eyelids   'you're
great'   they shout   as one astonished disciple
            which   calculated religiously   leaves
      room   so   'not frightened   (apart from)   I'm yours'

love song from the arboretum

since you stopped singing
I shan't be going down to the arboretum again
it has lost its leaves and the grass
marks grey time for winter

                    in your hide
you are playing solitaire
and the cards' black and white sepia is all washed up
piling on each other like dishes

                    this will be
the last winter before the graves open
for the Queen of Hearts   who will reclaim her children
and tell stories about how near this place was to perfect
before fashion found it and fate left her
for a game of poker   keeping only a dirty pink shirt   she lost
                                                        everything
and turned pale   there was an argument
but it was short as the protagonist flowers were dying
and anyway there's never much time left
                    before the florist . . .

now you are no longer eager to button-hole me with songs
and the birds are migrating
                    (you can still hear them tossing their wings
if you listen closely   but they have nowhere to go
so will not be back)

                    it's time to click my heels
and go to Kansas where it's open season on arboretums

    the songs are always the same
you can't escape them whatever arboretum you choose

the last you sang was that only the winters differ softly   you were wrong

                                           goodnight my love

I meant it all

www.ingramcontent.com/pod-product-compliance
Lightning Source LLC
Chambersburg PA
CBHW031933080426
42734CB00007B/662